LIGHT INTO BODIES

LIGHT INTO BODIES

POEMS

Nancy Chen Long

UNIVERSITY OF TAMPA PRESS

Manufactured in the United States of America
Printed on acid-free paper ∞
First Edition

On the Cover: Photograph by Nancy Chen Long.
Cover design by Nancy Chen Long, Joshua Steward, and Richard Mathews

The University of Tampa Press
401 West Kennedy Boulevard
Tampa, FL 33606

ISBN 978-159732-148-8 (hbk.)
ISBN 978-159732-147-1 (pbk.)

Browse & order online at
http://utpress.ut.edu

Library of Congress Cataloging-in-Publication Data

Names: Long, Nancy Chen, 1958- author.
Title: Light into bodies : poems / Nancy Chen Long.
Description: First edition. | Tampa : University of Tampa Press, 2017. |
  Includes bibliographical references.
Identifiers: LCCN 2017009007| ISBN 9781597321488 (hbk.) | ISBN 9781597321471 (pbk.)
Subjects: LCSH: Identity (Psychology)--Poetry.
Classification: LCC PS3612.O523 A6 2017 | DDC 811/.6--dc23
LC record available at https://lccn.loc.gov/2017009007

Contents

III

for my parents, who taught me the importance of language,

the power that attends it, and the isolation that can grow in its absence

Bodies burn and shine. Mountains take fire, the Caverns of the Earth are blown up, and the Sun continues violently hot and lucid, warms all things by Light. The changing of Bodies into Light and Light into Bodies is very conformable to the Course of Nature, which seems delighted with Transmutations.

—Isaac Newton, *Opticks*

On Seeing a Heronry of Egrets Nesting in a Tree

Perched ornamental like an angel
at the apex of a Christmas tree, the bird's neck is curved,
slender, the elegant sway of a tangent function.
The set of egrets—the score of them, nested as they are

in the treed twilight—they could pass as a scatterplot,
snowy ellipses on a dark Euclidean plane. I want to discover
a pattern, a sine wave to impose, dogmatic
order to instill upon their random arrangement.
               There is nothing

   more orderly than the number one,
                   is there? unity and identity,
like Euler's identity, numbers under the magical clutch
of an equation. When we mix every beautiful

number, it comes down to only one. When solving
for the irrational, there is no intercessory intercept
to invoke, no X in need of saving. On some days,

   my incantation is serial, primary,
                   a set of numbers I chant
recursively. It is a sacrament to count,
beadless. Beads being derivative, rosary or Buddhist,
beads in my hand are powder down, finely disintegrating

and clustered. To be celebrant in a wake of buzzards.
Is that heresy? To be one
            red-collared widowbird, mid-molt.
     In a volery of birds, to be identity

when all around us, the sutra of dichotomy, narrowing
      and scalar, some calculus of imputation, starlings
           seen as only black.

I

How do you learn to spell?
Blood, sky & the sun,
your own name first,
your first naming, your first name,
your first word.

—Margaret Atwood

Lessons

Every afternoon
        the woman my father hired
                would push
    the eraser-end of a yellow pencil
       into the mouth
of my mother

    to teach my mother
how to make a proper
        English sound.
  I would stand at the screen door
          of the Quonset hut,
      Okinawan-summer sapphire above me,
    twist the neck
       of the tiny green brontosaurus
   clutched in my hand,
and I would watch:

Blonde bouffant, cotton-candy hair piled high
        against my mother's straight black braid.
   Candy-apple lips, frosted eye lids
          next to a plain, topaz face.

No, no, *no*!
    and yet another press
  against the tongue,
      my mother, gagging.
   In her mouth, a stick.

Saving My Mother

Before he made his pilgrimage to the mountains
to become a Buddhist monk, before his red robes flapped
like prayer flags in the wind, before he embraced his own
neediness and raised his begging bowl to receive
another person's largess, my father was a generous man.
So begins my mother's story

of how religion saved her, the story of her father's
pre-monk generosity. He donated their clothes, shoes,
leftover food, sometimes the entire meal. And once,
even one of the family members. *My father was good for*
giving, my mother would say, *so generous with his property,*

which is how she repeatedly came to be the property
of another man. Over time, the story has changed.
When I was younger, her father had given
her to a certain man when she was six—
old enough to work—a gesture of kindness,
her father told her, towards someone unable

to have a child. Time and again, she managed
to get away, returning home only to be carted back.
And as my mother recounted the story, I pictured her
dropping grains of rice, marking the trail back home.

When I was older, it became commerce—the selling
of my mother. And each time she returned,
before sending her back, her father would beat her
with a bamboo cane to remind her how much better off
she was in any place other than home. Over time,

I came to realize that, unlike Hansel and Gretel,
my mother never did find her own way home.

Always, a man delivered her: the old fisherman
who found her one night stranded on a rock
in the sea, the quick passerby who snatched her

off of railroad tracks, train barreling down, moments away.
When she refused to work, the man himself would occasionally
return her, the way one might return

a defective plough. Her father would have to convince
the man to take her back. And so it went until the day
her father found religion in the mountains, the day he lost
his generosity, the day my mother said God heard her pleas.

Handiwork, or My Mother, Had She Not Married My Father

Would she have kept her self-made
promise—flee to America, find her fortune
or a safe place to sleep? I picture her
sitting cross-legged on the floor,

like she does even today, crocheting,
looping thin thread around
the flash of a silver needle.
I pretend she'd have other options

for escape as she mulled over
her sister's dislocated jaw, ribs cracked
at the hands of their father
for loving a man not of his choosing.

There would still be rumors of war
and she would keep that in mind—
what happens to some daughters
in times of war, repurposed

as comfort women. And when her friend's boyfriend,
a military man like my father, would again ask
"Do you plan to sell your handiwork in the States?"
I know she'd reply in her practical way

"I hear this sort of thing is now done
by machine." He would be mesmerized
as he watched the intricate patterns of lace
flow from her young hands over the curve

of her pregnant belly, heel of her unsanctioned,
half-American baby pressing against her spine.

A Fine Meal

i.
A fine Chinese meal,
my mother told me,
is made of five flavors,
a blending of elemental portions.

What is *sour*, she said, if not the flesh of plum?
> To know sour is to taste green
> watering across your tongue,
to feel the force
of wood striking your open palm.

How simple, *salt*, she said,
and how necessary,
married as she is to water.

And there, always, is *savory*, cavorting
with pungent and spice,
> lover in autumn, waiting,
> gilded under the iridescent harvest moon.

Child, proceed lightly with *bitter*, she warned.
(Who has not known its pinch?)
Cooling to the heart,
it favors full sun, its joy in fire.

Lastly, two kisses of *sweet*.
> Like a warm spell in winter,
> sweet should be used sparingly,
> for too much worries the earth.

Embrace all five, she said.
Repudiate not one.

ii.
A fine Irish meal,
my father told me,
is a *made* thing,

constructed with care,
(like the spire of a skyscraper
or the precision of a cesium beam)

concocted from what is available
(like that shard of blue limestone, jagged in your hand
and those mounds of cool moss, lush underfoot.)

      At the same time,
                 and with the same intensity,
an *inspired* thing,
           divined, he said—
               a happenstance of light thrown
                         by the Spirit
             or a sprite.
          Star seltzer effervescing across your tongue,
some nexus of intuition.

Place You Would Have Called Home

The good-luck door decked in winterberries,
on the right, the kitchen of babble, its alcove,
its clove and cayenne tea, the frigid air, ice
sheets on the window—as screen, as camouflage,

fireflies in the bedroom pulsing spyworks in code,
living room awash in purple—ironweed, milk thistle—

the nesting dolls nestled in rose hips on the mantle,
hair painted black peeking out among the pink,

doves in the dovecote, pigeons in the pie,
the ivied portico and the six Buddhas
—one on each step—rotund and laughing,

paper cut-out fairies guarding the garden, their white wings
bruised by the wind, chimes tinkling tin, the crippled creek,

two girls standing in a wading pool empty of water,
heads tilted skyward as they sing *Catch a Falling Star*
under a new moon, sheltered by the dark.

When We Finally Arrive Stateside,
My Father Gets Deployed to Vietnam

If you scarcely arrive to America,
just in time for first grade,
only to have your father sent away,
leaving you and your little sister

and your mother,
who doesn't speak
English, who can't read,
who trembles

all the time,
you won't remember him
leaving. You won't be able to

recall whether he left
after making you hot chocolate,
the way he did almost every morning
back in Okinawa,
or whether he slipped away at night
while everyone was safely asleep
or whether it was autumn
or whether you ever stopped crying—
because you said you would,
because you promised you'd be strong.

You certainly won't remember

if you waited with him
at the airbase, if you watched
the plane fly away,
waved as he disappeared,

then kept waving
to that empty desert of a sky
as if practicing
the stolid art of *good-bye*,
a skill you'd too soon grow to master.

But So Beautiful, Yes?

The silver foil tree with blue tinsel,
the oscillating light projected onto it,

       red yellow green,

the Barbie doll, with Ken accompaniment
—new and improved! with bendable knees—

the Japanese cartoon on TV, no sound,
a repeat: the immortal white snake-turned-princess,
     the man who loved her,

the gift my father sent from Vietnam
  to my mother, too beautiful
to open, in white
       paper with tiny poinsettias,
like blood red pin pricks on white,
but so beautiful, yes?

Yes, says my mother to my father's friend
   sitting next to her,
his reach for another
      mooncake, a melmac platter of moons
      on the coffee table.

Mahalia Jackson? no, Diahann Carroll low on the stereo—
         Some children see Him almond-eyed
         This Saviour whom we kneel beside—

the smell of rum in the man's coffee cup,
the way he looks at my mother,
my mother's lip, trembling,
her *Merry Christmas* murmurs,
fingers tight around mine.

Christmas, Saigon

Because children would run up
and throw hand grenades
into the bus filled with G.I.s
as it slowed to a stop, wire mesh
had been placed over the windows.
My father would watch
one particular child—not unlike
his own eight-year old—as she darted
towards the bus on sultry afternoons,
grenade in hand, reaching as she jumped,
her sapling fingers struggling
to place the fish hook
attached to the end of the grenade
onto the screen—not unlike
the gesture his own child made
in a snapshot sent from home,
his daughter arching up
as she secured an ornament
onto a blue spruce.

Before the Days of Self, or Elementary School Achievement Test as Primer

A child will learn to check
herself, mark the correct

answer, press the sabered
lead, requisite #2,

will fill in the hole,
will fill in the whole

square so no white
is left.

*

Regarding achievement
tests, the question

below the student name
will be answered

by the teacher
who will instruct them:

"All children are to color-
in *Caucasoid*." Except three.

Those children she will call out
by name. Pointing to the first child,
"You are *Mongoloid*."

*

A child will sprint across
the small patch of Mojave Desert

between a grade school
and trailer park,

will apologize to her father
for having denied

him on a test, will apologize
for having failed
to achieve Caucasoid.

Laying to Rest in a Field of Bluebonnets

A child made her own way once,
down a caliche road, until she was far

from home, skipping past home
after abandoned home, winding through

another sparse trailer park,
until the road grew more crumbled,

the Texas brush that lined it, more virulent.
Roiling clouds the blue-black hue

of a bruise rose up along the horizon,
distant, like a long line of lost sisters

marching their slow pilgrimage across the sky.
Sometimes the child could hear

the staccato mock of a bird perched
on a field post, the heady rush of the Colorado

as it bent near. Then there it was—
knee-high sea of flowers, wild and blue.

She knelt, and, for a moment,
appeared to be genuflecting.

But hers was more the movement
of a battle crawl, belly hugging the ground

close, low so no one could see her.
Hands and knees scraped, she kept crawling

until she reached the center.
What she will remember most clearly—

how the bluebonnets smelled
both flowery and weedy,

how the soil, teeming with insects,
felt inviting and alive. She lay there

for hours in the arms of wildflowers,
surrounded by blue, safe

in a blue flower-coffin, waiting
for rain. She prayed, not for the sprinkled mercy

of a drizzle, but the Rubicon of a deluge,
legions of grackles and hawks circling overhead.

Dislocated

Mother and Father fly past, tossed
about, along with the sofa, the stove,
Sophie and her catnip mice, the potted cactus—
all requisite characters and habiliments
of family, all going up, up, up the tornado.
Mouths open, but she hears only
Sophie's steady purr. For nights,
for days, she sees the tornado, chalk marks
on the sidewalk, cyclone,
bodies prone on linoleum, twisted
episodes syncopated.

It's Whatever You Make of It

their first pet was a Siamese cat
cold and standoffish

like her mother
her father always wanted

    Siamese cats
            both perfect
            and imperfect
   her parents
         who obeyed the stand-in
     pinch-hitters
for god
   said it's easier
   to command the flesh
   rather than control
               the mind
               they said
               it's whatever you make of it

What Some Things Are Worth According to Her Grandfather

Any job worth doing is worth doing right.
And any right worth having is worth

a fight. Remember, though, fighting
like cats and dogs is for the birds, while a bird

in the BBQ pit is worth two in the bush.
And any bush worth beating around

is worth its weight in glitter, even though
all that glitters is not worth a penny.

Gee, how many times have I told you,
a penny for your thoughts—

well that's just worth bull (but not the kind
of bull that goes off half-cocked

like a gun in a china shop.) Speaking of shopping,
shopping is therapy but only if you learn to say no,

because no one's island is worth a stick in your eye.
A stick in your eye, ya say? Don't forget:

An eye for an eye pulls the whole world up by the roots.
And everyone knows the root of all evil has no secrets.

Besides, a secret's only worth keeping
if it's as pretty as a picture, since a picture sells

a thousand stories, and a good story makes the world
blow up. Surely, what goes up must be worth

double time and time is money, so take that fork
in the wall. Yes, walls have ears, but no voice

to spill the beans. And a hill of beans
is just one thing after another. But another needle

in the haystack, well, now that's worth a second look.
Of course, what looks and quacks like a duck

is the wrong man for the job! And we all know
any job worth doing is worth doing right.

How She First Discovered Sex

Only grown-ups can do it. Kids aren't allowed. Even in second grade,
she understood there were things her parents couldn't tell her until she

was older. But it was Saturday night, and again there were giggles
and rustling noises coming from her parent's bedroom and there was that

light streaming from under their door, where she lay on the linoleum
floor, peering through the crack. She couldn't see a thing. So she slid the door

open just a sliver. And what did she see? Candy wrappers strewn all
about the bed, her mom and dad propped up against pillows, chuckling and

munching, reading the Sunday funny papers. It was quite a coup to
get a hold of the Sunday funnies on Saturday, thanks to the

neighbor, a newspaper man, who came by every evening with the next-
day's copy—the same neighbor who got her dad a job at the local

tile factory. Seeing her at the door, her mom patted the bed. *Hop
on up, sweetie*. And she did, snuggled in between her parents as they

read the funnies to her, shared Almond Joys, licorice twists, Tootsie Rolls.
So this is sex, she thought, *eating candy in bed. One of those fun things*

only grown-ups are allowed to do. It turned into a ritual
every Saturday night until eating candy in bed became known

as Saturday-night. Her favorite: Sky Bars, four squares of chocolate, each
with a different gooey center. She liked the busyness inside of

the chocolate. And, of course, Bit-o-Honey. *Do you want some Saturday-
night?* her mom would ask as she broke open a bag of fine confections.

Gonga

Her grandpa calls her to tell her about some travel gonga, that's what he says—
    gonga—which she promptly googles while he's still talking to her, and she sees
it's another word for pot, though pronounced differently, a word favored
    by those older stoners who had their heyday in the 1970s. But her Grandpa isn't

an old stoner—he's a genteel man in his 80s who lives in a nursing home,
    so she figures he must be saying GONG-a, you know, like the sound
a gong makes when someone wins some wonderful prize. *Let's go to Ireland,*
    you and me and your great-Aunt Margaret, he says. *There's this great gonga*

if we travel in the next two weeks, and she pictures herself puttering around Ireland
    with an old man who has Parkinson's who shuffles instead of walks
and an even older woman with emphysema in a wheelchair who carts
    a canister of oxygen around, and herself, who waddles,

being seven months pregnant, and she thinks, *Well, I can handle that.*
    But then she imagines herself in the airport, standing in an endless
line, with her big belly, and her mind flips back to the time she flew in 2002,
    when airport security meant a ten-hour wait: She had entered the terminal

with a wave of others. Some of the folks were juggling luggage, others
    were juggling children and the blonde in front of her was coddling a guitar case
and clunky ski-tubes. They were told to go to the end of some line, but she couldn't
    see the end of any line and then a uniformed man pointed to this twine

of humanity that undulated and zig-zagged all the way through the terminal,
    so everyone followed that coil of humanity out into the parking garage
and then along the entire length of the garage, and then out into the street,
    where finally, she saw the end of the line. And with every step they took,

their din of sighs grew louder until she heard the same refrain being sung into a sea
    of cell phones: *I'm going to miss this flight!!* But it gets worse,
because once they were appended to the line end, they settled into this sluggish
    peristaltic movement, micro-inching towards baggage-check kiosks

and ticket-counters and each second stretched longer and longer until she was sure
    she had caught demophobia. This guy from Tupelo started joking about last rites
to make her feel better, but instead she took to screaming *MY RIGHTS*
    ARE BEING VIOLATED! WHERE ARE MY RIGHTS?! over and over

until the Zen monk gave her the sly, one-eyed, side glance to please be quiet.
    So they ended up chatting, those outside of the parking garage,
and first it was how's-the-weather sorts of stuff, then folks started sharing
    personal info and they each weighed in on the pros and cons of natural

childbirth for the edification of the blonde with the skis, who was considering
    artificial insemination. Somewhere along the line, though, time snapped.
They became denizens of a Candid-Camera universe, delirious in the belief
    that they were part of a joke, some comic sketch. This had to be a joke, right?

Hope became a slick-haired announcer popping out to restore reality. They kept
    searching for her, for Hope. Was she hiding behind that Volkswagen?
Yes folks, they knew she'd say, *you have been X'ed.*
    Now look this way, please—and smile into the camera.

Suddenly she hears a shriek coming from the other end of the phone
    —*Smoke 'em if you got 'em!*—and it's Periwig, her grandpa's parakeet
yanking her back to the present. She knows her grandpa's waiting for an answer
    about the gonga. She toys with the idea of saying no. Then she thinks

Well, he's been in the States ever since Nana died—this could be his last chance.
    Even so, she's leaning towards no because she's not big-hearted and selfless
like her cousin Seamus. She comes up with an excuse related to being pregnant
    because who could hold that against her? And just when she's feeling

justified, she feels a kick, hard right beneath her heart, like the baby's telling her
    to get one—a heart, that is. *Sure Grandpa,* she hears herself say.

Hold on Lightly

She's never held on
to anything tightly.

As a child, her hand
would slip readily from

that of her father's.
Running towards the school bus,

her blue-plaid satchel
would simply drop from her

grasp. At her first job,
as a waitress, trays fell

and tumblers tumbled.
Even today, her grip

on reality—
feather-light. You can pull

it away from her
with the softest tug.

II

The balled
Pulp of your heart
Confronts its small
Mill of silence

                    –Sylvia Plath

Haibun: Honeymoon on Mackinac Island

Through the open window of the suite comes the saccharin scent of fudge, an acrid whiff of horse piss, and the ripe stench of horse manure. I leave my husband sleeping on the heart-shaped bed to take a morning walk. The street is empty, except for a solitary, bedraggled street-cleaner who is shoveling piles of scat into a wagon pulled by two mares, and a queue of blindered horses that line both sides of the mile-stretch of town. Wailing ghosts and ghouls and the lonely moan of a pipe organ emanate from the Haunted Theater. I round the bend. Darting towards me, a mongrel, haggard. Firmly clenched in its teeth, a fresh deer leg. Next to the white picket fence of a mansion, also white, is the remainder of the carcass. Above it, vultures kettling. Close by, gulls strut and squawk. They scatter as a bridal party whizzes past sounding the tinny clang of their bike bells. Behind her like a flag of surrender, the bride's veil, streaming.

perched on a white cliff
a falcon calls out
empty sky

Murmuration

A patch of black silk undulates against the amber evening sky. I pull over in a field, watch it swirl. As the silk-patch approaches, it pixelates into a thousand starlings, with more joining each minute. The fabric-flock changes shape seamlessly as if of one mind: A thin black snake-shape expands into a black river, billows into a spiral, only to reverse and compress into a tight black ball. Then—Big Bang!—the ball explodes and reshapes into a giant boomerang that hurls towards earth like a kamikaze pilot, at the last second dividing into two huge black swans. The two swans dart away from one another, then turn and dart back towards each other. They crash into a thunderous splash, a black ocean wave with starling-droplets falling from the crest. The droplets waft back up to the unified flock—a collision with no casualties. Starlings cut a swath across the horizon until they own the whole sky and their wings sound like rustling wind. Finally, they take to earth, settling in trees, covering the field around the pond. One lands so close, a bird about nine-inches long. After all the black, my eyes are startled by such color: a yellow-tipped beak, an eerie green that shimmers off of feathers soft around the head and throat, an opaline-purple sheen along the body, torso-feathers dipped in white, wing-feathers outlined in bronze—and those legs, those very sturdy red legs.

Wingspan

The puma, stalking. And though the ceiling
is naught but night sky, the room

is made of red glass—eight walls ten-feet tall,
the sliding door, the bolt—all blood-colored

and glass. Homing pigeons flutter around me,
doting. Like angels. I have named them.

Monarch. Swallowtail. Lacewing. *Come sing to me*
I coo, while the black puma paces. My body

is frocked in blue. I wear a brood
of *Lycaeides melissa samuelis* like a bridal veil,

my hair laced in forget-me-nots.
Sometimes, when I'm perfectly still,

a pigeon will mistake me
for an electrical wire, perch long enough

for me to seize its spindly feathers,
attach a message, set it free.

Inflamed

The man at our table, his insistence
last night—how the color red will conjure
up feelings of rage, as if to see red
is to see rage. How logical, I thought

Fire color + blood color =
boiling blood. Rage, a simple slip in-
to those familiar ways of being. Dare
we break them? You want to—the way you broke

that flawless Lalique vase you thought so rare
in its redness, smashed against your mother's
antique vanity, crystalline no more.
Your grandmother's face, helpless to stop you,

drained of color, save her pencil-thin lips
glossed in red—like the red of that northern
cardinal you're always searching for. Look—
lucky you! Such a bird is lighting right

now onto the lower branch of this sweet
gum tree next to our bench in the park. See
how it disappears in the autumnal-
red star-shaped leaves? I like how the cool nip

of the biting wind reddens the apple
of your cheeks. Is it too cold for you? Oh,
you and your fascination with red. Here,
sip this red rooibos tea. It'll fire

up the caverns of your heart, ruby like
Santa's suit in that photo, when we were

in Florida, fake snow, fake tree with all
red lights, flashing, spin, spin, flashing red lights

of the ambulance that Christmas our child
was taken to the emergency room,
so tiny on the gurney. No one dies
of scarlet fever. You asked for a sign.

Remember your father's words? *It will be
fair weather, for the sky is red*. So true,
the sanguine sky that night, but all I could
think about was the rusty dust of Mars,

whether heaven was a scarlet desert
with polar ice caps. At least we could pick
out the planet from among the others.
How lucky that it is so visible,

lucky us, lucky red, lucky like me,
nubile bride in a crimson dress, gift-wrapped
in red, the bittersweet door to our house,
lucky—your birth, my birth, our child's. So let

us wave our red flag of complicity.
Yes, tonight let us sip our favorite
aperitif. Like that Campari, we
also have dark-red bitters and secrets,

we who carol of luck and of splendid
weather, we who sing with rage in our throats.

Heading Home

there is the tree of not-knowing and what is
not knowing
if not an accident
waiting to jolt open the dark
road you have always traveled
familiar in its curve

take for example the curve of a husband's back
take the sycamore tree in the bend
its gray-and-white mottled knots
trunk too close to the road
trunk camouflaged lost in the snow

there is no berth on a country road
no grace granted by a berm
it's late and field after flattened field
moon lights up the snow
each oddly-shaped flake does its job
reflecting refracting
if you were awake you would say something
how fireworks have grown out of the ground
how there is the unknowing
the cannot know
and either the baby is safe in the car seat or she isn't

if you had been awake
you would have seen the herd of deer
stalking through the cornfield
stepping through stubble that peeked above all that whiteness
to you it would have looked like something stolen
from a manger scene
birth of a child on a country road

star from afar portending something significant
perhaps deer instead of cattle
the snow glitter on a Christmas card

there is the unknown
and there is the choosing to not know
the choice to drift
and so you drift

off the road
there is the incomputable
long division
timbre of a heart divided by slivers of sycamore

there is the language you cannot parse
true and false are all there
is a deer in the road there is
a sycamore tree trunk
wide as baby's cradle
waiting for you

Dugong

i.

What strange fascination she holds
for men, the sand-colored sea cow:

                                called *lady of the sea,*
           mistaken for women
           reincarnated, inspiration to the legend-
ary mermaid.

Where her ancestors once foraged for tender green shoots
                                as mammals of the land,
she now walks on flippers, nibbling the delicate seagrass
                                that sways in an ocean meadow.

Poised on her sturdy tail,
           she hoists her bland head out of shallow salt water,
                 gasps to fill her elephantine lungs with air.

ii.

Once, in Thailand, there was a young wife
who had a vigorous affection
for seagrass fruit. As her cravings escalated,
she wandered each day deeper into the sea,
lingered longer in the buoyant brine.

One day she didn't come home.
Her husband, steadfast, searched for her
until the night that she visited him
in a dream, saying she could never return

to land. Now half woman, half fish,
she met her beloved one final time,
then returned forever to water.

iii.

My husband again tells me about the mystery
woman he spotted
      swimming across Brunei Bay.

   When I hear him say
"At first, she was just a vague form
      in the cove—," I think of Isaac Newton,
         who knew of *no Body*
less apt to shine than Water.
I know my husband did not see me
      as a woman until I came closer.
I know the way my pale flesh glinted

            in the sun, he believed me
     to be naked as I approached
    just shy of land.

And when he saw me abruptly
thrust my head out of water,
gasp for air, and turn

to ripple back, deeper into the sea,
I know he lost sight of me.

Lapidary

It's only in October that a rock collector will uncover
a problem in her masonry work—a birthmark

or hardhearted mar, some telltale cicatrix that consumes
her attention. She needn't chisel very far

in the house she built
to find at least one lapillus buried

in the sheetrock. Always that jagged piece
of rubble needing to be unearthed,

a tumbling rough she insists must be sanded
and ground over and over and over

until she is able to finally feel
it. Smooth enough to swallow.

A common stone herself,
she often inspects the same wall,

one widely distributed across many rooms.
Take, for example, the shared wall

of the living and dying
rooms where one wouldn't expect

to be able to excavate
a heartful of malachite.

I can think of no greener stone,
she might say. *It reminds me of the greenest grass,*

wouldn't you agree? For her sake, let us say *yes*.
From her mouth, the rock collector might manufacture

a hand or a heart, a north or a south, beliefs
that seem to bear true for a decade.

We are not fooled. We see she is stone—
masked, holes for a mouth and a heart—a green

that shines for a few years, maybe even ten.
But her heart is still just a hole.

Only the most excellent quarries, she'll say.
Isn't a stone worth living for?

Tell her it would be a mistake. Tell her
in ten years, she'll be like all of her walls—pocked

with holes. She'll demand proof.
It's only then that you should take her

to the garden on the other side of town,
where the two baby stones sleep

side by side, both with their polished marble
hearts, their malachite mouths,

both swaddled in the greenest grass.

On Seeing "The Embroiderer, or Mette Gauguin"

After the divorce, I took a class in art appreciation
to occupy my head. We studied Gauguin.
While everyone else was taken in by his use of color
and image after image of nude Tahitian beauties,
I couldn't stop staring at his wife Mette, embroidering.
I'd seen it before, as a painting of a woman
in obedient domesticity.
Now, she was a wife *in situ,* posing
while her husband withheld the sun

to blot out her face. He rendered her featureless.
She became more mask, a quiet interruption
in the wallpaper. Instead of needlepoint,
I started to imagine that she would have wanted
to leave, stroll down the banks of the Seine,
smolder along the soot-like evening,
reclaiming that textured glow some of us feel
as we fall under the whitewash of summer.

I scarcely glanced at the other paintings,
those fine features of Tehamana—
the Tahitian who became, at fourteen, mother
of Gauguin's youngest son, whom he named Emile,
after his oldest son Emile, who lived in France
with Mette. The day Mette learned of his pubescent
other-bride must have been trauma,

the way it is when you learn of a husband's lover,
the way it is when a girl comes to your home
on a Sunday afternoon in August
while you're outside gardening

and you think it odd
that the dog seems to know her
as he trots up the driveway to greet her,
and the weight of summer humidity
has caused you to be slushed in sweat
and you smile politely as she approaches.

Overhearing at the Café

Outside, sweet gum leaves
    shiver like red stars,
        in the breeze—

a million tiny shudders,
    each one tethered
        to its own small branch.

It's all about perspective.
    Someone is talking
        about Michelangelo,

his *Creation of Adam,* the brilliant
    foreshortening, so real
        looking. As I sip my coffee,

I realize—I never noticed.
    My eyes see only the gap,
        how God leans in, stretches

to the very tip of his index finger,
    how he looks as if he's trying
        harder than Adam

to bridge the distance,
    all those angels and putti
        holding God back.

Adam looks unimpressed.
    He knows the world
        will soon revolve around him.

I dreamed once of the world
swirling, too, around me. God
and I floated among the stars

above Earth as it exploded.
God held me
back as I jetted towards

the destruction. After the flames died,
I flitted about,
scooping up every bit

of stardust that remained. God watched
as I patted it back together,
silent witness

as I recreated a world
—so real looking—
out of spit and green dust.

Tanka

—then the dream scattered,
images swept away
by the morning wind:
me, crouched in the root cellar,
the man, screeching, his gun, jammed.

Riven

Through snow, over
ice, he peddles
his bicycle
down the street towards
a laundry mat,
duffle bag filled
with dirty clothes
balanced on his
back. Turning the
corner, he rides
past the small house
where he once lived.
On the porch, he
sees his estranged
wife smiling. And
there, behind her,
closing the door—
a man he does
not recognize.
And there, on the
stranger's shoulders,
his child, laughing.

Reunion: Day 3

You turn my palm over
looking for a life line. "Another shot?"

the waitress asks. She reminds me
of my mother, who, like you, had a brother

lost to war. Three refills
of coffee later, you attempt a laugh

and say "For the first time, I think I feel
safe." I picture that frayed photo,

black-and-white, your father,
a boy almost, stationed in Vietnam,

head shot, close up.
Empty pack of cigarettes

strapped to the front of his helmet,
the words *'Lucky Strike'* on his forehead,

the concentric circles of the logo—
a bulls-eye. Your father's stare
into the camera, a dare, a wish.

*

We cut through the clear,
kayaking at a swan's pace,
use the small curved sail
when the wind is opportune,

pushing behind us. Hours
spent circumnavigating
the summer we had
before your first deployment:
picking berries, the nettles
my reach would always find—a sting
unbearable for such a small thing
as a touch.

Headfirst, we dive
into the bubble-springed water.
When we first kiss, you whisper *peach*.
The taste of peaches. On your skin,
the hint of an orchard.

*

"I might re-enlist," you say.
I nod, understanding

what it is to crave
a thing that kills.

The beach at midnight.
I think I hear the haunt
of a loon across the lake, faint.

Free

I watch you
skipping through
lemon-colored tulips,
blond curls
bob with each hop.
I used to be a champion skipper
when I was six you yell back to me.
Your voice trails off
as you bounce farther
and farther away into spring. I watch
as you turn around

and beam at me through the dust
of high-noon, proud
in your fine skipping style.
What luck I am your play-date
I think as you bound back to me,
so nonchalant
about what others might think
of you, a grown man
who dares to skip in daylight.

Orion

His body is a freckled map of the night
and I can kiss each constellation

here in this bed beneath a summered window,
even now—at high noon—when the light of all real stars

is washed out by just one sun, the broad
whitewash of day. Sunlight falls across his belly,

exposing Orion, who is no heavenly shepherd,
but hunter pointing the way to the dark

huddle that is Pleiades, cluster of specks located
near the soft small of his back, splatter of spots

near the scarred scalpel wound.
My fingers read the scar's ridges

as if they were Braille, a trail that takes me back
to a month of living in a white waiting room,

hospital pool of blinding light,
hot pot and instant coffee in the corner.

When I close my eyes, I can still count
the number of daisies in the faux-wood frame

over the black vinyl couch where I would curl up
each night in the arms of a hospital blanket,

reread the same issue of *Astronomy*,
looking for constellations to touch.

He Takes Up Carving

He's been rummaging in the woods all week, scavenging
for the straightest pieces—rods of red oak, ironwood,
sassafras saplings—peels back the bark, sanding for hours,
then inlays intricate patterns of blue lapis, honey-striped

tiger's eye, turquoise. Sometimes a compass recessed
into the top. Using his father's engraver, he outlines pines
and cabins, the occasional deer, and always his initials
into each stick. They're the reason why he's hauled those boxes

up out of the basement—to clear a small work space.
Basketball cards catalogued by team and year, scores of plastic
cowpokes with no cows, a Hawaiian silk shirt, some army fatigues—
all transferred to the garage to make room for these walking sticks

sculpted and reshaped by his hands. Over sixty canes now,
arranged by size. Her head on his shoulder while he reads
another book on wood-carving, she daydreams of the last time
they parasailed, holding hands as they soared above Lake Huron,

before he was laid off, before he had his long blonde curls
shorn like sheep's wool, before he renamed himself
Gottlieb. Curled up at their feet asleep, their Australian shepherd
lets out a whimper, paws twitching as if running. Yesterday,

the dog ran circles around her, nipped at her heels, darted back
and forth, barking as if to say "Go this way! No—go that way!"
herding her along the path from the backwoods. Such an urgency to it—
that need to be of use.

Tanka

Listen, that gobbling ...
Wild turkeys? We chase the sounds
downstream. No—gray tree frogs,
courting. So loud!
Even louder, our laughter.

III

She said, "Empty, The Word is a wind in the trees.

Full, it is the voice of a woman
reading out loud from a book of names."

– Li-Young Lee

Dot Product: The Cross Between Particle Theory and Pointillism

Ø

Up close, everything is made up
of elementary particles, tiny dots.

They vibrate, shimmer, dance wildly.
 Maybe because they're agitated,
 maybe they're excited,

it doesn't matter.
 The countless tiny particles
 that make us and fill us
 are moving, always moving,
even if just a quiver.

ω

At a distance, anything
 of any shape
will look like a dot, a mere point.

An insignificant dot risks
 being missed

unless it is named.
 And so those who explicate
 have given a name—*point particles*—
 to the near nothingness
of our elementary dancing dots.

And the explicators say
            those point particles at the root of everything—
                idealized—they have no structure,
                have no mass.
                They take up no space.
Up close
   then, perhaps nothing
   can look like a dot
   because there is no
thing to see.
              And yet—
here we are. We, who are made of quivering particles,
      we have mass.
           We take up space.

$\aleph_1$

      At a distance, a huddle of dots
will take shape, will take color.

Take pointillism: a technique of painting
      that uses countless numbers
of colored dots, distinct and unblended dots
      all on the flat plane of a raw canvas.
Point after point of pure and different color.

        When viewed from afar,
           the dots will be marshaled into solid shapes
                    by the mind:
              perhaps into the shape of a proper parasol
          held by a woman,
        a bustled woman,
       prim and detached,

a monkey at her feet,
a dog romping by her side.
In the distance, a boat at full sail,
white, billowy.

And those dots, perhaps a division
of blues, purples, oranges, and yellows,
will converge and blend into some other color—
let's imagine into the fragrant green of a grassy field.

Form and color, forged
from the smallest dots with no structure.

$\aleph_2$
At a distance, God is a pointillist painter
and time a ready canvas.

At a distance, the universe is a painting in one of the art galleries
and evolution a paint-by-*point particles* adventure.

At a distance, humanity is a palette of constrained color
and I am one dot, dancing wildly.

Curry

On my skin lingers
     the scent of coriander
and cardamom, ginger
     and fenugreek, a hint
of clove, perhaps cayenne.
My hands yellow
     with turmeric.

When I was nine, I mixed a similar
     concoction with rice vinegar,
     boiled it down into a magic potion
     to douse on a patch
of wild cane. That Texas weed
was supposed to sprout overnight
     like the fabled beanstalk—my ladder
to God, whom I called
     M81 at the time.

Now I boil the spice mix
     with coconut milk,
pour it over bean thread,
     what my mother calls *dōng fěn,*
winter powder, my Indian rendition
     a betrayal
of her prized recipe.

*

In the photograph, my mother
sits atop a black horse bareback,
snowcapped mountains
     behind her. She is younger
     than I am now, barefoot,
her jeans thread-bare.

I imagine her a Sherpa,
    or a distant descendant
of Empress Börte, instead of a barmaid
    in British Columbia.

A small boy, beaming,
stands next to the horse,
    clutching a curry comb.
In another photo,
    he and my mother are combing
        the horse,
their backs to the camera.

    I imagine the two
are laughing.
    They sound like
        wind chimes,
        soft in September,
that quiet time
        just before the trees
drop their leaves.
    But that was a time
before. A brother I never knew.

*

The mower drones in the background
as one of my sisters tends
    our mother's lawn.
    The smell of cut grass
always reminds me
    of Texas,
a hot green, weed smell.

Out on the porch,
          my brother,
fawning all over
          our mother, clutches her
hand as if she were the one
     drowning. He raves
about her prized dish,
     so much better than any
of her daughters'. My youngest
     sister, threading
Buddhist prayer beads
     at the kitchen table,
     steals a sideways glance
at me. Our brother,

     ten years absent,
     reappears, seeking
ever more favor
from our mother,
     as if being the only son
among a pentacle of daughters
     were not favor enough.

Accommodation

Tenant, if home can be called an invention, then why not invent one?
        Say yes to a kitchenette, but leave behind the plates
piled high with errors in judgment,
                              your sink filled

with lessons of scarce.
Invent one outside of persistent wishing.

           Though you quote Milton,
you think of sweat and so you reek.   O Outcast, don't drink
    your heartfelt thanks   out of the stammer of a lie.
One way to raze a dream is to say   *I am a patch on shame,*
               an unworthy plume.

       You need no witness   to your patchwork
of a dream   home, your sweet invention   on the edge a bluff.
You need no consent to sound.   So speak your mother tongue,
    say your history.   Must you always have a light to put on?

The Cleave of Color

puce. i know that	it's a little like purple, or similar kind of
color. a little boy once said	dream
it to me	when we get older,
—we were coloring—	our petals blanched
in a field of bluebells	—our ancestors chanting in our memory
under the beam of a chestnut tree:	*we are all one, child.*
i, who had drawn a cart-wheeling girl,	preferring to be insular,
i didn't want to color her.	humans graft color with artifice and so
i wanted her to be white.	what is real seems real if some other says it is.
there is no white	washing our imperfections,
silly, the boy said to me.	intellect may say we are vapor, while experience says
but you are	to stay the course, even though nothing can be seen except
white	flecks against a foreboding sky. stay the course,
i said,	even if happiness should look like a point, even if
looking at his timberwolf	skin betrays the truth. what can be said about the
eyes and tumbleweed	dispersions of words, chaos and form—they are
shadows. he shook his head. no one is	ad infinitum—
white. i am peach and	our options being finite, then
you are maize. to prove it,	let us broaden our palette—
he raised the crayon to my skin	in order to honor the original—
and the color disappeared against me.	yes, this is so like a dream. and so
i gasped. he did not know	there is no cold, there is only distance from the sun. change
the rules. let's race, i said. i'll race you to	the boundary of
the purple house.	what is considered home,
he said, but	those many rooms in one mansion, spinning,
racing	hurling through space. this picture
makes no sense	—a single stone in a galaxy of stones—
and besides, it's not	the only thing that matters. the flash of
purple, it's puce.	form is flesh, the imprint of color.
to prove it, he searched	through archives of memory,
everyplace	where we once danced to some familiar chant
trying to find it.	—still, it hums, ambient, steadfast.

Continual Process Improvement for the Astute Young-Adult Student, or Lesson as Lesion

i. Lessons

    a. A person is a process—"Overview of Constructive Developmental Theory"
    b. Education (the development of a person) is a process—*Scouting in Practice*
    c. a definition of continual process improvement: the seeking of small
       improvements in processes ... with the goal of increasing quality
    d. Quality is in the eye of the beholder—*Harvard Business Review*

ii. Hypothesis Based on Lessons

If quality is a goal
and goal a destination,

then to follow the sun
is to be perfect

in navigation,
is to arrive perfectly

at your destination.

iii. Testing of Hypothesis / Early Application of Lessons

if you don't do better
someone else will

see an opportunity
and they will be right

where you thought
the sun would be

the sun ought to be
shooting its solar flare

into the shiniest part
of your hummingbird heart

heart quaking
with its brummagem
bastion of quick-flitting flicks
its flurry of flutters

heart that doesn't beat
in its nest
because beating has buried
within it a rest

and rest is a flaw
an invitation

to transgress
a breach in your porcelain
defense strategy

kerneled with a fear-seed
of tremble

solitary seed in the fallow field
where you knot-nest

you fear-weary
feathered thing you

full of waiting
for the sun
waiting for the sun to teach

you look sunward
watch-wait in stare
stare-follow the sun

to learn how
exactly how
one can improve

the lot of her skin
how she might better be
the blanched perfection
she's been taught

she must be blanched
in perfection

she must be perfectly blanched
she must be whited out

The Importance of Shells

Water beads
  down my back. I peel
    off my poplin blouse.

Weighted with sweat,
  the t-shirt underneath
    sticks to me

like flypaper. Flies buzz
  about plastic pots heavy
    with tomatoes

rotting on the vine. My mother and I
  sit on lawn chairs
    and the plastic webbing cuts

into my thighs.
  In front of my mother's trailer,
    the only oasis of green

is turning brown-tipped, toasting
  under the late-autumn sun,
    grass coming to mimic

the color of cracked earth.
  Afternoon heat breaks through
    the sulphur-colored

catalpa leaves that shade us.
  My mother's face, aging bleak,
    streaked with sweat.

Oh, we are like peas in a pod,
　　　we two, with our full-moon
　　　　　faces, hair black

and hands quick with purpose.
　　　Our hands that carry
　　　　　a small harvest, unexpected.

Peas, out-of-season.
　　　My mother says she can grow
anything from a dead stick

and I know she means
　　　it's the living
　　　　　that flummoxes her.

We are shelling
　　　those surprising peas.
　　　　　Seashells decorate the edge

of her patio—because to shell is to shed
　　　and to shed is to be light
　　　　　like the sun. And my mother

likes the word *like*,
　　　the way it imitates.
　　　　　The way a word is like a box,

the way a box is like a house,
　　　the way she is like pebblesnail
　　　　　fashioning a tiny house

to carry on her back.
  Such a tiny house
    can carry no burden.

Like a box full of memories,
  that house holds her days, life
    flecked with bits of dream.

Because if one's life
  is like a box,
    one can hold it

with both hands,
  feel the heft of it
    weighted with earth.

Meditation—Home as an Extension of Body

Some days, home is a bastion,
body-shield bunker, granitic

host within which to huddle, tomb-
worthy extension of my flesh—surely

no wolf could wind it. Today, home
is a river running breathless, fluid

vagabond, loyal to no one place.
All one and yet not. River.

Not the riverbed, not the confine,
rigor-mortis press of clay.

Rather—rush that carries,
skin-bare and bobbing.

Exposed and yet not. Body.
And yet absent of body.

River Is a Verb When Home Is Stopgap

          Home in a dust bowl.   I plunge
both hands in   and sieve sand   through my fingers
          sifting for rock. Confucius,

sitting at the kitchen table, sips gunpowder
tea. *Tsk tsk*. He pats my hand   like a father
    of philosophy.   *Time flows away*
like the water in the river, he says.   He knows

it's not the water—it's the dust that throws me.
        I once read *a river*
never rests. Or maybe it was *when one's home is a river*
running dry,   *each moment is spent bleeding*

into the next.   Whatever I read has not helped.
      Now all of my time is spent sanding
every rock until there is nothing
left but dust.   It's risky to run

a river dry.   The full moon might fit inside.
     And then where would you be?
In a river bowl   with a mouth   full
      of moon dust.

    But Confucius does not judge me.
He knows where the water pools,   promises
we'll visit   someday. In my dreams,

I make a home out of mud
                from a bog near the mouth of a river.
I am rivered and succulent in my dreams,
work the humus with my whole body.
                                In my gardens,

sundews and pitcher plants flourish.
Dust is never an option.   I have no need to hide.

Retreat

one day   of silence
     at a convent
others in the group think

about Mary   I think
               of Emily
Dickinson sequestered
               in a way
silent

    *

      so much more white here
      than farther north   so much more

winter

    *

      There.   There it is.
The knock at the door—lucid? lucre?
Any door will do.

Pray.

    *

Overthink—underfeel—overspeak. Underneath
      a flood of cover, it is too easy,
               too narrow, just this

    *

the fullness of all hope
I plant in empty air
just a grasping

Dark Night Offertory

I who am here dissembled
Proffer my deeds to oblivion.
                    — T. S. Eliot

I give to you: all
of my treacle trinkets,
every name I ever made
for myself, one mosaic
of flesh imposed
with ash, adorned
with a mask of pyrite.

Savior

Thunder, O God. Sound
a boon that bellows

like the brass toll
of a black hole. Send,
O God. Send us

a godsend, *unanointed*
blaze to be manumitter

of us, of rust,
firebrand to disabuse,
pyre, cremator to incinerate

our every righteous hoard,
our every underbrush
urge to prey.

The CommonWealth, Cash and Carry

Everyone   sells out. Someone somewhere
            is shilling. Ammunition
sells like water

falls—careens like a creek flows.
Never straight.   See? bullets
ricochet   homebound.

            In the streets, a wealth of well-
armed children fills our shoes.

Marksmen. Listen!
our moonlight serenade—
the howl of coyotes.

Auctioned, we are fat now,
content, with our pistols cocked.

Color Sights

The gun convention is a hit, over seventy-five thousand
in attendance, flooding our city with much needed
tourist green. It's noon and a bell rings

throughout the convention hall, an invitation for all children
to head to center stage so that they can ring
the one-ton freedom bell made of well-balanced bronze.

We head towards the bell.
Down one of the aisles, a display of Gun Luxe
jewelry—earrings, necklaces, rings

made with a kaleidoscope
of semiprecious stones and freshwater pearls,
made from spent bullet shells and rifle blanks.

A fresh-faced woman—nineteen, maybe twenty—
with a bright, toothy smile
mans the booth. She wears pink shorts and a pink shirt

stylized with two sparkling pink guns over the words
Be Calm and Carry On. Down another aisle, under a large
American flag hanging from the display, is a poster

of the president hanging on a pole,
a poster intended to be a shooting target.
On it, the president has been transformed

into a zombie, flesh falling from his bones.
There's a bulls eye over his forehead, another
over his heart. And beneath the poster—

a matching mannequin, a three-dimensional target
of the president with green skin, white zombie eyes.
Blood drips from his mouth, as if it were evidence

of the signs around it
heralding *This target bleeds*
when you shoot it.

"The Flowers That Never Fade"

Leave the land, take
the winter. All men die,
a nation of withering
leaves. Garland
in the hour of death, we begin
even now to wear flowers.

A Drift of Dust

I

Because clay is not the genesis of our bodies,
    because it is light that bodies us forth into form—
our shapes shift.
             We scatter
like a cluster of motes ruffled by a trifling breeze,
      interstellar dust dispersed by a gust
  of wind, like the one
that cuts through us even now, on this cold paper-night

when air is ice. Countless nights I have stayed up
to name the leaves I'd collected: sycamore, ginkgo,
cottonwood, willow—pressed them into yellow
      paper, trying to preserve
their shape. But all leaves lose shape,
disintegrating into glints of dust. Everything appears
to reduce, molder into a pile of particulates.

II

No, a drift of dust cannot hold a shape. It must be held.
I once tried to hold a shape, imposed a form
                 onto my own self,
molded the flitting flakes of me into the shape of a hole,
so that I could fit onto a twig. I wanted to attach
to the end of a stem—to be a leaf among leaves,
to cling to the branch. There I clung until the day I became breathless,

      choked from the source.
My clutch, weary from the wind, weakened and I fell, turning
      earthy and sweet, intoxicatingly light with decay.
And as my shape shifted, it seemed all that held me
together was my name.

III

If we are but ash, then let our names be the urns that hold us,
     skins we slip into—the garments that shield us

from the wind. Because wind cannot help but concuss the fine particles
of our little-lived moments strung together.
     And we cannot help but scatter

the light that forms us.
More space than shape, these bodies, this ocean of cosmic dust.

She Timbers Her Faith with Cedar

The voice of the Lord breaks the cedars ...
The voice of the Lord twists the oaks
and strips the forests bare.
—Psalm 29

Witness her hands fretted with splinters,
    cottonwood pollen falling
        from her lashes like a nuisance
           rain. Poison-oak
              spokes once anchored her

doppelgängered heart to the pedestrian
    gods of a stranger's ancestors.
        Poppied rituals. Terracotta temples.
        She mistook their gangly bones
           to be arrows in a quiver.

But like spectral drops of water,
    their lexicons evaporated,
        leaving babble, salt, silt. Notice
           from such tumbleweed vernacular
              sprouts her own homiletic seedlings—

broadleaf, conifer, coral. She authors
    her own scaldwood of proverbs.
        Today, each winter nightmare becomes her.
        A dead promise resurrected:
        She has named herself

after her silenced father's dead mother.
    Half-sister to the moon,
        umber-colored and amber-foamed,
        she's steeped in tannins
           leached from swamps of cedar.

"Blazing Black Holes Spotted in Spiral Beauty"

1.

                                        Outside this window of the nursing home
where my father lives, snow cascades
like sheets of gauze. I can make out only edges. Today,

                                everything I know can be outlined
with an Etch-a-sketch, erased. My father's latest
surgery has left him with a patched left eye. Even

                                 with one good eye, black
holes are what he sees, letters missing
from the alphabet. Everything cusps

                                edgeless. Small pills blink
in and out of sight as he studies them,
color-popped like M&Ms, red yellow green;

                                with a shift of a gaze
slightly to the left, suddenly he sees
a blue capsule. Shifting to the right,

2.
it vanishes. When I was a child,
   my father gave himself many names.

Dictionary Don, when we played Scrabble.
   Later, he was *Maldendo Vestibule.*
Because he liked the sound, he said.

   But even then I knew he was branding
himself with place. *Malden,* town of his birth.
Vestibule, narthex to the self.

I am where I began. When I was thirteen,
    he told me he was adopted
when he, too, was thirteen. His last name,

    not really his. We were stargazing
in an abandoned horse pasture, searching for M81
in Ursa Major, that Great Bear, our close neighbor.

3.
Nose pinned against the pinepost of the pasture fence,
my appaloosa has cornered herself

again, flanked by barbed wire. On her snowy hind quarters,
a splatter of black spots clusters like the Pleiades. Night

blind, she simply stands there, seeming to sway
in the indigo evening light. I watch her, wanting to kiss

her forehead like a child. If only my eyes would stop
watering, I would paint the plastic stars glued to my ceiling.

Better, I would blaze a geodesic dome out of glass,
let the stars paint themselves above me.

4.
    "So black holes are magenta!" my father exclaims as I read
to him the news of spiraled galaxy IC342, of its two black holes,
    newly-seen blazing spots of magenta. Black translated
into pink. Color granted to the nothingness
    of a hole. In the Mojave desert, I once searched

the constellation Fornax for the cosmic eye, NGC1350—
    galaxy spiraling larger than the Milky Way. But I couldn't see it
through the telescope. "Avert your vision," the star-guide told me.
    As I looked away, it came into view
in my peripheral vision. How faint it is, oblong cosmic eye.
    We are deceived into believing

5.

          an outline can be the whole
       or love cannot be a number
            or a shape
       is something less than a name.
"Everyone should have a number
      of names like my father,"
    I once said to a man I'd just met. In black chiffon,
drinking Maker's Mark, neat, I told him
         "The Wolf Moon is my friend."
"No," he volleyed back. "You
    are the moon, good
only for reflected light."
     Luna, he kept calling me as if he hoped
      the name would stick
me into a corner.
      "Luna," he slurred, "you speak
         really good
     English. What are you,
Mexican? Eskimo? Indian?"
   I confess there was a time I may have been grateful,
      having early earned
the right to be mute. I'm not

6.

sad, although a little boy once thought I was.
He was shaping his family on an Etch-a-sketch,
scraping away gray with a magic stylus
to expose their dark bodies. Reaching out
for my hand—as if we shared a secret—
his small palm tender ebony, he asked
"Are you sad because you want to die?" "*Die?*"
"So you can go to heaven." "*Heaven?*"
"So you can be white. Everyone in heaven is white."

7 .

With the shift of a gaze—it may be the outline that changes
    or it may be the name.

        Maker, why brand me
as a byword? You have made me

marginalia in a book of names. Father, spot me
    so that I may better see   water crystalizing into sheets   of eyelet,

so that I may shed this moonblink. Sweet appaloosa,
    we both know that to blind
                is to corner. *Light*
into bodies | | woman into bird.

Our shapes, spiral. Our names, as numbered as the stars.

Occupying Fear

Back then, fear tasted like mist.
                    The color of drizzle, it sounded
like the stillness before a storm—wanting
                to soothe, yet longing
to be the monsoon.   In that previous era
I was named

Docile Teacup, deferential porcelain funnel-
form containing the formless

water and wind.   Now I am called Tempest.
Fear sounds like a shock wave that I need
            to obliterate before being
obliterated.   The color of blitzkrieg,

it tastes of the fire of war—consumptive,
            the funeral pyre of my slow cremation.
            In the next era,
I will name myself.

Notes

The manuscript's epigraph by Isaac Newton is from *Opticks: or, A treatise of the reflections, refractions, inflections & colours of light*. Based on the 4th ed., corrected. London, 1730. pp. 349, 399. *Project Gutenberg*. www.gutenberg.org.

"'Blazing Black Holes Spotted in Spiral Beauty':" The poem's title is the title of an article on NASA's website (www.nasa.gov). The phrase "light into bodies" is from *Opticks* by Isaac Newton.

"Dugong:" The phrase "no Body less apt to shine than Water" is from *Opticks* by Isaac Newton.

"He Takes Up Carving" is indebted to Susanna Childress' poem "Weaving" from her book *Entering the House of Awe*.

"How She First Discovered Sex" is based on a story I was told while travelling with my father to visit his childhood sweetheart, whom he hadn't seen for over sixty years.

"Inflamed:" The epigraph "It will be fair weather, for the sky is red" is from Matthew 16:2-3.

"She Timbers Her Faith with Cedar" combines original work with individual words sampled from poems in issue 33.1 of the Australian journal *CORDITE: THE REMIXES*, which allows reuse through the Creative Commons license. The following poems were sampled: "Simply by Sailing in a New Direction," "You saw me first Isabella," "Doppelgänger," "Garden Piece," "Beautiful," "inadequate stovetop," "Kerb side collection," "apropos," "Dogs in Space," "Ways of the Mind as Subject 46-60," "Just Lexicons," "Litany," "Loki," and "The Walker."

"Accommodation" is a remix of text on pages 58, 599-604 of *Guard of Honor* by James Gould Cozzens. NY: Harcourt, 1948. "Remix" is defined here as the scrambling of a portion of text within a source, including phrases, individual words, and new words not actually in the selection, which are discovered by applying erasure to a word or phrase.

"'The Flowers That Never Fade'" is an erasure. Source "January 5th –The Flowers That Never Fade" from *My Daily Meditation for the Circling Year*, by John Henry Jowett (1914).

Acknowledgments

I owe much to many and am overflowing with gratitude. Beginning close to home: As always, thank you to my parents and children for their unconditional love and support. For gracing my life with ceaseless patience, love and inspiration, and for believing in me, I am deeply and inexpressibly grateful to my husband David Hitzeman.

To those who got me on my way: I am indebted to Susanna Childress for her steadfast encouragement and for helping me find a well of courage and to Cynthia Bretheim for pointing me in the right direction. Heartfelt thanks to Catherine Bowman and Alyce Miller for their support. I am grateful to the Women Writing for a Change of Bloomington community, especially to Beth Lodge-Rigal for her encouragement and her unassailable faith in the process of writing and in poetry.

Unending gratitude to Spalding University's Brief Residency MFA program for providing a place I will always call home. Thank you to my Spalding mentors and workshop leaders— Jeanie Thompson, Greg Pape, Debra Kang Dean, Randall Horton, Maureen Morehead —for their essential guidance and support, and to Molly Peacock and Kathleen Driskell for their invaluable guidance with the first version of this manuscript. For their vision and leadership in developing and maintaining the remarkable Master of Fine Arts program at Spalding University, I am beholden to Sena Jeter Naslund, Karen Mann, Kathleen Driskell, and Katy Yocom. Each one of you is dear to my heart.

To my poetry family of friends in real life and online—thank you. You sustain me and continue to enrich my life as well as improve my poems. I am blessed to know you.

Thank you to the Provincetown Fine Arts Work Center and the fine folks at 24PearlStreet, especially Ada Limón, Nancy Pearson, Peter Campion, and Tim Earley.

Gratitude to Sandra Simonds for her careful reading and in-depth comments on the manuscript and to Sandra Beasley and Kelly Nelson for critiquing versions of the manuscript.

Heartfelt thanks to the editors of *Tampa Review* for selecting this as the winner of the Tampa Review Poetry Prize and to the University of Tampa Press for publishing the book. Special thanks to you, Richard Mathews, for your patience, wisdom, and all that you do.

Grateful acknowledgment is made to the editors of the following publications for first publishing the following poems, sometimes in different versions:

Alaska Quarterly Review, "On Seeing 'The Embroiderer, Or Mette Gauguin'"

Big River Poetry Review, "Hold on Lightly"

Blue Lyra Review, "A Drift of Dust," "He Takes Up Carving"

The Briar Cliff Review, "Orion"

Boxcar Poetry Review, "Reunion: Day 3"

Cold Mountain Review, "Lessons"

Crab Orchard Review, "Saving My Mother"

Elsewhere, "Dislocated"

Mason's Road, "When We Finally Arrive Stateside, My Father Gets Deployed to Vietnam"

Naugatuck River Review, "How She First Discovered Sex"

Ninth Letter, "Christmas, Saigon"

Noctua Review, "Haibun: Mackinac Island"

Paper Nautilus, "Dot Product: The Cross Between Particle Theory and Pointillism"

Penumbra, "Dugong," "Inflamed"

Pith Journal, "'The Flowers That Never Fade'"

Pleiades, "The Common Wealth, Cash and Carry"

Poor Claudia, "Continual Process Improvement for the Astute Young-Adult Student, Or Lesson as Lesion"

Referential Magazine, "It's Whatever You Make of It," "Retreat," "She Timbers Her Faith with Cedar"

RHINO, "But So Beautiful, Yes?"

Superstition Review, "Lapidary"

Sycamore Review, "'Blazing Black Holes Spotted in Spiral Beauty'"

Tampa Review, "Murmuration," "Laying to Rest in a Field of Bluebonnets," "Handiwork, Or My Mother, Had She Not Married My Father," "Overhearing at the Café"

The Wabash Watershed, "River is a Verb When Home is a Stopgap"

The Louisville Review, "Curry"

Two Hawks Quarterly, "A Fine Meal"

Weave Magazine, "The Cleave of Color"

Zone 3, "Heading Home," "On Seeing a Heronry of Egrets Nesting in a Tree," "Wingspan

"Accommodation" was first published under a different title in the chapbook *Clouds as Inkblots for the War Prone* (Red Bird Chapbooks, 2013).

About the Author

Nancy Chen Long was born in Taipei, Taiwan, to a Taiwanese mother and an American father who was stationed in Taiwan as a linguist for the U. S. Air Force. The family lived primarily in Okinawa before moving stateside when she was six. Once in the States, they moved every couple of years until she was a teenager, at which time they settled in Fort Wayne, Indiana, a non-military town where her father served as an advisor to the Air National Guard.

While creative writing was Chen Long's first choice for a major, she was strongly counselled to major in science instead. Plans were made for her to attend the National Taiwan University and major in biochemistry. However, it was not to be. Due to intervening life circumstances, she didn't enroll in college full-time until her mid-twenties, when she majored in Electrical Engineering Technology. After completing her degree, Chen Long went on to pursue an MBA and develop a career in technology, working as an electrical engineer, software consultant, and project manager before taking a position at Indiana University in 2005.

Later in life, through the encouragement of friends and professors, Chen Long went on to pursue the MFA she had originally wanted as a teenager, graduating from Spalding University in 2013. She is a 2017 NEA fellowship recipient and author of the chapbook *Clouds as Inkblots for the War Prone* (Red Bird Chapbooks, 2013). Her first book manuscript was selected as winner of Tampa Review Prize for Poetry in 2016. She lives in south-central Indiana with her husband and works at Indiana University in the Research Technologies division.

About the Book

Light into Bodies is set in Joanna and Perpetua digital fonts developed from types designed by the English sculptor and wood engraver Eric Gill between 1925 and 1932. Perpetua was commissioned for the British Monotype Corporation by Stanley Morison, and it, especially, shows the influence of Gill's handcrafted chisel lettering in stone and wood. As Morison wrote, "The finely bracketed serif with which the sculptors of the Roman inscriptions dignified their alphabet is symbolic; it signified their sense of the fundamental difference between private and public writing; between script and inscription. . . . The fine serif is not in origin calligraphic but epigraphic; not written but sculptured. It follows that a set of drawings of a finely serifed type by a contemporary practioner of lettering could best be made by [a sculptor], and Gill was the obvious man to solve it." The type seemed especially appropriate for this book, in which the poems bridge private and public writing and move gracefully through both script and inscription. Gill designed Joanna in 1931-32, naming it for one of his daughters, and reserving it for exclusive use by his printing shop, Hague & Gill, which he ran with his son-in-law, René Hague. He chose Joanna to personally typeset his 1931 book on type and page design, *An Essay on Typography*. The title page of *Light into Bodies* includes a decorative leaf adapted by Joshua Steward from a woodcut ornament by Gill for his 1931 edition of *The Four Gospels*. The book was typeset and designed, in collaboration with the author, by Richard Mathews at the University of Tampa Press.

Poetry from the University of Tampa Press

John R. Bensko, *Visitations*◊

John Blair, *The Occasions of Paradise**

Michelle Boisseau, *Among the Gorgons**

Bruce Bond, *Black Anthem*°

Jenny Browne, *At Once*

Jenny Browne, *The Second Reason*

Jenny Browne, *Dear Stranger*

Christopher Buckley, *Rolling the Bones**

Christopher Buckley, *White Shirt*

Richard Chess, *Chair in the Desert*

Richard Chess, *Tekiah*

Richard Chess, *Third Temple*

Richard Chess, *Love Nailed to the Doorpost*

Kevin Jeffery Clarke, *The Movie of Us*

Jane Ellen Glasser, *Light Persists**

Benjamin S. Grossberg, *Sweet Core Orchard**

Benjamin S. Grossberg, *Space Traveler*

Michael Hettich, *Systems of Vanishing**

Dennis Hinrichsen, *Rip-tooth**

Patricia Hooper, *Separate Flights*◊

Kathleen Jesme, *Fire Eater*

Jennifer Key, *The Old Dominion**

Steve Kowit, *The First Noble Truth**

Steve Kowit, *Cherish*

Lance Larsen, *Backyard Alchemy*

Lance Larsen, *Genius Loci*

Lance Larsen, *In All Their Animal Brilliance**

Julia B. Levine, *Ask**

Julia B. Levine, *Ditch-tender*

Nancy Chen Long, *Light into Bodies**

Sarah Maclay, *Whore**

Sarah Maclay, *The White Bride*

Sarah Maclay, *Music for the Black Room*

Peter Meinke, *Lines from Neuchâtel*

John Willis Menard, *Lays in Summer Lands*

Kent Shaw, *Calenture**

Barry Silesky, *This Disease*

Jordan Smith, *For Appearances**

Jordan Smith, *The Names of Things Are Leaving*

Jordan Smith, *The Light in the Film*

Lisa M. Steinman, *Carslaw's Sequences*

Lisa M. Steinman, *Absence & Presence*

Marjorie Stelmach, *Bent upon Light*

Marjorie Stelmach, *A History of Disappearance*

Ira Sukrungruang, *In Thailand It Is Night*◊

Richard Terrill, *Coming Late to Rachmaninoff*

Richard Terrill, *Almost Dark*

Matt Yurdana, *Public Gestures*

* Denotes winner of the Tampa Review Prize for Poetry
◊ Denotes winner of the Anita Claire Scharf Award